Rupert Matthews
TYRANNOSAURUS
Illustrated by Colin Newman

Language Consultant:
Anne Smith, BA
Dinosaur Consultant:
John A Cooper, B.Sc., AMA, FGS

PUFFIN BOOKS

Tyrannosaurus

Rupert Matthews
TYRANNOSAURUS
Illustrated by Colin Newman

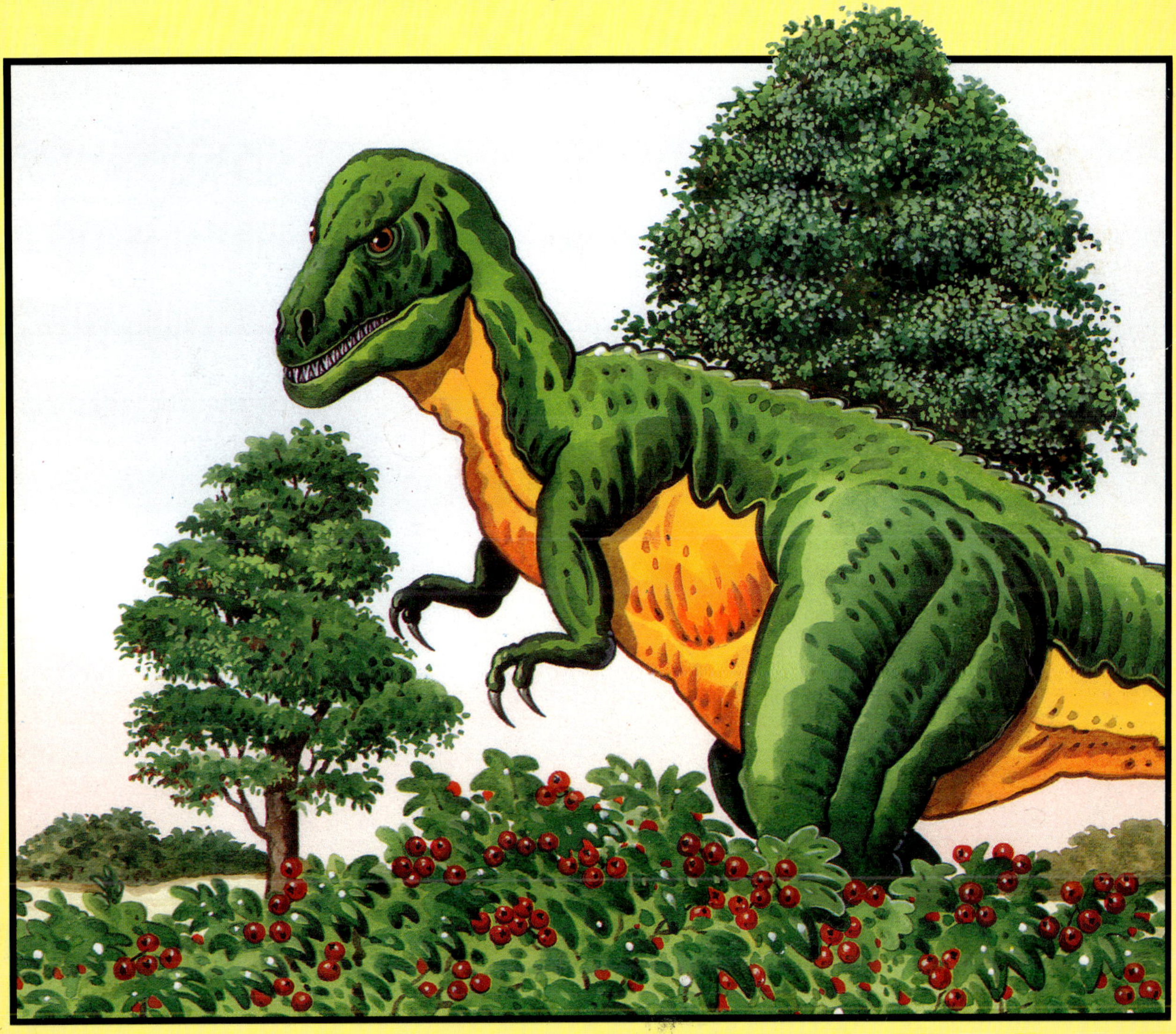

Would you run and hide if you saw a Tyrannosaurus?

You would after discovering the many incredible facts about this ferocious meat-eating dinosaur – where did it live? Why was it so fierce? How did it fight? And with whom?

Find out more about these prehistoric beasts through this easy to read text and colourful illustrations.

Tyrannosaurus was a very fierce dinosaur. Other dinosaurs ran to hide when they saw Tyrannosaurus.

Corythosaurus

Tyrannosaurus ate other dinosaurs. He was so big and strong he could fight any other sort of dinosaur.

When another dinosaur came by
Tyrannosaurus would attack it.

Tyrannosaurus

Then there would be a fight. If Tyrannosaurus won he ate the other dinosaur.

Corythosaurus

Tyrannosaurus fought with teeth and claws when attacking other dinosaurs. His teeth were longer than a pencil and were very sharp.

Tyrannosaurus lived in North America about 70 million years ago.

Tyrannosaurus was the biggest meat-eating dinosaur. He was over 12 metres long and 5 metres tall. He was bigger than an elephant.

A baby Tyrannosaurus hatched out of an egg. The babies hunted for lizards and birds.

Tyrannosaurus liked to live alone. If a stranger wanted to live on Tyrannosaurus' land they would have a fight.

Then, one of them would give in and move away.

Tyrannosaurus lived with many different kinds of animal. There were birds, lizards and snakes, and a few small animals like rats and mice.

No Tyrannosaurus is alive today. But there are animals which behave a bit like Tyrannosaurus. The fiercest of these is the tiger.

Tiger

Some other Picture Puffin Fact Books

AIRCRAFT	SEASONS
ANIMALS AT NIGHT	SHARKS
ANTS	SNAILS
BUTTERFLIES	STICKLEBACKS
CASTLES	SUNFLOWERS
COLOURS	TRACTORS
DINOSAURS	TRICERATOPS
DUCKS	TRUCKS AND TRAILERS
FROGS	VISIT TO THE FARM
MONSTER MACHINES	WHALES
OUTER SPACE	WHAT CAN I SEE: IN THE FIELD
RABBITS	WHAT CAN I SEE: AT THE SEASIDE

PUFFIN BOOKS

Published by the Penguin Group
Penguin Books Ltd, 27 Wrights Lane, London W8 5TZ, England
Penguin Books USA Inc., 375 Hudson Street, New York, New York 10014, USA
Penguin Books Australia Ltd, Ringwood, Victoria, Australia
Penguin Books Canada Ltd, 10 Alcorn Avenue, Toronto, Ontario, Canada M4V 3B2
Penguin Books (NZ) Ltd, 182-190 Wairau Road, Auckland 10, New Zealand

Penguin Books Ltd, Registered Offices: Harmondsworth, Middlesex, England

First published by Firefly Books Limited 1990
Published in Picture Puffins 1992
10 9 8 7 6 5 4 3 2 1

Text and illustrations copyright © Firefly Books Limited, 1990
All rights reserved

The moral right of the author and ilustrator has been asserted

Printed in Italy by Printers srl – Trento

Except in the United States of America, this book is sold subject to
the condition that it shall not, by way of trade or otherwise, be lent,
re-sold, hired out, or otherwise circulated without the publisher's
prior consent in any form of binding or cover other than that in which
it is published and without a similar condition including this condition
being imposed on the subsequent purchaser

TYRANNOSAURUS

Rupert Matthews

Illustrated by Colin Newman

U.K. £3.50
CAN. $5.99

PICTURE PUFFIN FACT BOOKS

ISBN 0-14-054384-8